D0266881

Hand in Hand

Emotional development through literature

Judy Hunter • Stella Phillips • Noreen Wetton

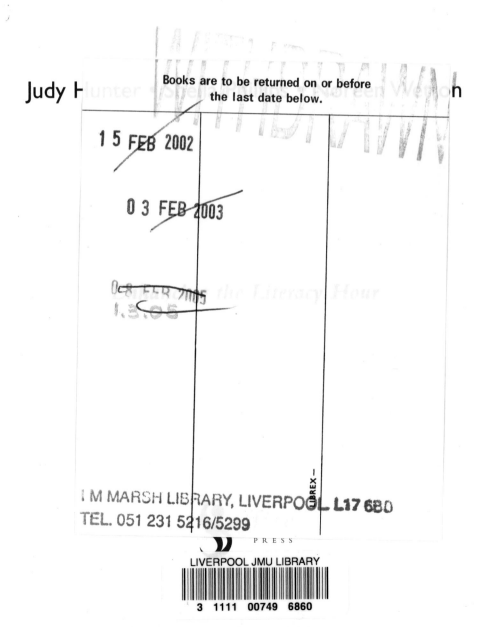

... the Literacy Hour

PRESS

Extract from 'The Velveteen Rabbit' by Margery Williams reprinted by permission of William Heinemann (a division of Egmont Children's Books).

Edited by Susan Norman
Cover design by Julia Vinton
Book design by Hugh L'Estrange
Illustrations by Mike Phillips
Clip art by DeskGallery, Zedcor, Inc

Printed in Great Britain by Progressive Printing (UK) Ltd

First published July 1998

Published by

Saffire Press
34 Park Hall Road
East Finchley
London, England
N2 9PU
Fax +44 (0)181 444 4693
email hugh@saffirepress.co.uk

ISBN 1 901564 03 7

Hand in Hand

Emotional development through literature

ABOUT THE AUTHORS

Judy Hunter and **Sheila Phillips** worked together for several years in the education sector before moving into private training and consultancy. As 'Wilson-Elliott, Training and Consultancy', they work with a wide range of organisations both nationally and internationally. Particularly close to their hearts is the belief that education should give children opportunities to develop emotionally, by offering them a language which allows them to express their feelings, skills which will enable them to form respectful personal relationships, and the self-knowledge and beliefs to cope with difficult situations and life events.

Noreen Wetton is a parent, grandparent, school governor, former teacher, teacher trainer and head teacher who is addicted to listening to and learning from children. Previously Director of the HEA's Primary Health Education project, she is now Senior Research Fellow in the Research and Graduate School of Education at Southampton University. She has written and lectured extensively, and is co-author of *Feeling Good – Raising self-esteem in the primary school classroom*.

The authors and publisher welcome comments on their publications.

For further information about training on educational issues, contact
Wilson-Elliott, Training and Consultancy
72 Ewesley Road
High Barnes
Sunderland, England
SR4 7PR
email judy@wilsonelliott.demon.co.uk

CONTENTS

About this book

This book is about getting the most out of the literacy hour. It is about developing children's love of literature and comprehension of text. It is about enjoyment, and increasing children's knowledge of what language can be. As they become familiar with talking about the feelings and emotions in stories, the literacy hour becomes a wonderful opportunity to explore and talk about personal and sensitive issues.

Literature can provide a unique setting for the exploration of the issues children see as sensitive, and for developing a language which enables them to express their feelings freely and confidently. Children can talk through the characters, which is often safer than talking about themselves directly. As we, the readers, set out through a book, we are sharing not only the narrative, but a whole range of basic human emotions. We experience together the characters' feelings and relationships, we get inside their problems, applaud (or not) their decisions. We learn with the characters as they make discoveries about themselves and the world around them.

Together, in a book we can be taken into situations beyond our day-to-day lives. We can be afraid with, and for, the characters, laugh and cry with them, hold our breath with them, be surprised and angry about the way they behave. We can be a step ahead of the characters, seeing the dangers before they do, knowing how the story will end before they do. We can experience it as if it was happening to us, safe in the knowledge that it is 'only a story'.

Children can visit places that we would not and could not take them to in reality, places where they can explore feelings. They can face dangers in new worlds without threat or fear. After all, it is only a book and a book can be closed.

The issues that children see as sensitive and affecting their well-being are often very different from those which adults consider sensitive. Children's sensitivities stem from their need to be unique while not being different from others, to be valued as valuable people, to be secure and unthreatened, to be listened to. They want their feelings to be acknowledged and valued: their feelings about growing and growing up, about separation, parting, loss, death, about leaving childhood behind, about love and loving. They struggle for words to describe frustration, empathy, delight, jealousy, hope, isolation, uncertainty, conflict, remorse, fear and joy. Their language might be limited, but their feelings are as complex as any adult's. Through literature, we and they can find the language to talk about their feelings, as we move forward together, hand in hand.

The structure of the book

Hand in Hand is organised around a series of themes of relevance to children's emotional development. For each theme, a variety of titles is recommended and the first two are used as the basis of example lessons for the literacy hour. Usually, one of these texts is aimed at younger children (❖) and the other at slightly older ones (❖ ❖), although many of the books have layers of meaning and subtlety that can be appreciated at different ages or by children at different levels of emotional development. You will know your classes.

The material gives a focus for comprehension, style, use of language and opportunities to introduce metaphor, characterisation, first and third person narrative, plots, and the ways stories can be developed. Different techniques are suggested including whole class work, individual and group activities and coming together again for reflection and evaluation. Most importantly, in every lesson the story or extract is read through without discussion, and at the end read again without stopping for comment, in order to preserve the unity of the story itself and focus on that key ingredient – enjoyment.

This book is just a starting point. We hope you will adapt the lesson format and tasks to the other suggested texts, or to other books on your shelves, and go on from there to develop your own lessons. Our aim is to help children feel comfortable with the literacy hour sessions and get them used to the routine of sitting quietly and immersing themselves in the marvellous world of literature.

In short, we want to get them hooked on books!

We pay tribute to the many
authors and illustrators of children's literature,
without whose wealth of talent and creativity
this book would not have been written.

Extract from *The Velveteen Rabbit* by Margery Williams

'What is REAL?' asked the Rabbit one day, when they were lying side by side near the nursery fender, before Nana came to tidy the room. 'Does it mean having things that buzz inside you and a stick-out handle?'

'Real isn't how you are made,' said the Skin Horse. 'It's a thing that happens to you. When a child loves you for a long, long time, not just to play with, but REALLY loves you, then you become Real.'

'Does it hurt?' asked the Rabbit.

'Sometimes,' said the Skin Horse, for he was always truthful. 'When you are Real you don't mind being hurt.'

'Does it happen all at once, like being wound up,' he asked, 'or bit by bit?'

'It doesn't happen all at once,' said the Skin Horse. 'You become. It takes a long time. That's why it doesn't often happen to people who break easily, or have sharp edges, or who have to be carefully kept. Generally, by the time you are Real, most of your hair has been loved off, and your eyes drop out and you get loose in your joints and very shabby. But these things don't matter at all, because once you are Real you can't be ugly, except to people who don't understand.'

This book is about stimulating children intellectually,
encouraging them to love literature
and helping them to understand their emotions.

It is about 'becoming real'.

THEME ONE
BEING ME, BEING YOU

Learning together, learning to be together

Celebrating differences, uniqueness, similarities. What makes me 'Me'? What makes you 'You'?

Lesson One
❖ *Six Dinner Sid*

Setting the scene

This is a story called 'Six Dinner Sid'. Try to make a picture in your head of someone who eats six dinners every day.

Show the children the cover of the book which will make it clear that Sid is a cat.

Focus

At the end of this story I want you to tell me how Sid knew what kind of a cat to be with his different owners. I also want you to listen for the words which told you how Sid behaved.

Share the text with the children without discussion.

Comprehension

How did Sid behave differently in each house? Why? How did he manage to keep his secret?

What words can we use to describe Sid and his different owners in the different houses?

swanky

rough

tough

naughty

silly

suspicious

furious

Style and use of language

Where in the story did you know that Sid was going to be found out? Which words gave you a clue?
[eg Life was just about perfect.]

12

Link with personal/ sensitive issues Ask the children if there was any moment in the story where they were worried about Sid, about his health or about him being safe. Raise the issue of too much of anything, eg food and medicines.

Individual, pair or group work
- Ask the children how they behave differently in different places and situations, eg classroom, playground, home, visiting someone in hospital, going to a party, etc. Collect words to describe how they feel in different places.

CLASSROOM	PLAYGROUND	HOME	HOSPITAL	PARTY
quiet careful	noisy	comfortable	nervous	excited

- Draw pictures to illustrate some of the feelings listed above. Add captions.

- Choose from the list of feelings and write sentences about times when they experienced that feeling.

  I felt excited when ....

  I felt nervous when ....

Reflection Bring the class together to share their work.

Ask the children how they can become more like the people in Pythagoras Place – people who talk, share and are friendly towards each other.

Learning together, learning to be together

 Re-read the story.

Lesson Two
❖❖ *Comfort Herself*

Setting the scene   *I am going to read you a short extract from the story of Katie Comfort Jones, a girl who had a long way to go.*

Give a summary of the story so far:

Comfort Jones was born in England where she enjoys school and her family life. When her mother dies she has to decide whether to go to Africa to live with her father in Ghana, or stay with her English grandparents. She goes to Africa where her father, Mante, leaves her with his mother in a village far away. Comfort Jones has to learn to live a quite different life, to be a quite different girl, to be obedient, not to ask too many questions. One evening, in the family hut she hears someone saying it will soon be time to find her a husband.

Focus   *At the end of this reading I want you to think of the feelings Comfort had before she told her grandmother what she had decided and how she felt when she had told her.*

Pick up the story towards the end of Chapter 10 from, *'Soon it will be Comfort's turn to find a husband'*, and read to the end of the chapter.

Comprehension   *What words describe Comfort's feelings before and after she told her Grandmother her decision? What words describe Grandmother's feelings?*

What made it so difficult for Comfort Jones to tell her Grandmother?

What did Comfort mean when she said, 'Comfort Jones you've a long way to go?' Did she mean in miles, or did she mean something else about her own problems?

How do you think the story ends?

Explain a *'been to'* boy - ie one who has been to England.

Comfort tells Grandmother

Style and use of language *Explain the language used to describe how Comfort spoke her real feelings. Does the language help us understand how she felt? How?*

In a short extract, the author managed to paint a picture of
(a) Comfort with her new hairstyle
(b) Grandmother
(c) the atmosphere in the hut. How did she do this?

Re-read the description of Grandmother, especially the use of the **simile** *'gnarled wood like the figurehead'. How does it help to create the picture?*

'... made of gnarled wood like the figurehead of some ancient ship'

'... like a cork wedged in a bottle'

Consider everyday expressions we use which compare one thing with another, eg as clear as ..., as cold as ..., runs like a ..., floats like ... . How do they help the listener understand what we mean?

It might be appropriate to teach the word **simile** along with the concept here.

Link with personal/ sensitive issues Discuss the importance of Comfort's statement, 'I belong to myself'. What did she mean? Remind the children that each of us is unique. We all belong to ourselves, and we can all make our own decisions even if it isn't always easy. You could relate the statement to peer pressure, peer choice and the difficulties which can occur when people want to belong to themselves and to one or more groups at the same time.

Individual, pair or group work
- Ask the class to devise similes to describe a scene or situation, such as a group of people frozen in surprise, a playground covered with early morning frost, a traffic jam.
- Ask the children, working in pairs or small groups, to devise a scenario where someone is saying, *'I belong to myself'*.

Reflection Remind the class that they have all shared Comfort Jones' decision-making process, but that they are all individuals too, sharing some feelings and experiences, but having their own unique ones as well.

Learning together, learning to be together

 Re-read the extract and make the book available in the classroom library.

GROWING AND GROWING UP

Learning to relate

Me growing, you growing, growing up together in a changing world.

SUGGESTED LITERATURE

Once There Were Giants
Martin Waddell   ❖

Once there was a baby in the house, and to that baby, Mum, Dad, Jill, John, and Uncle Tom were giants. But, little by little, the baby changes, grows and develops in many ways until she becomes a giant too. A story of the family cycle.

Penguin's Progress
Jill Tomlinson   ❖❖

Otto is a penguin chick, but he is different from all the other chicks he knows. He is 'first chick', the first penguin born that year, so it's his job to look after all the younger ones as they grow up. But nobody has told him what 'growing up' means, and life is both confusing and exciting.

Growing Pains
Jenny Stow

It's hard trying to be a rhinoceros when you have no horns. Horns take time to grow says Shukudu's mother. Shukudu learns patience and eventually gains his greatest wish.

Nearly But Not Quite
Paul Rogers

Simon doesn't feel at all like the big boy everyone tells him to be. He looks around at the big house, the big lawn and the great big trees, and feels quite, quite, small.

Emma's Lamb
Kim Lewis

Emma's father brings home a little lost lamb. He's wet and cold and hungry. Emma wants to keep him and look after him herself, but in her heart, she knows that the lamb needs to be with his mother. As the lamb grows, Emma grows up in her understanding of the lamb's needs.

The Gorilla Who Wanted To Grow Up
Jill Tomlinson

Pongo is a young gorilla who can't wait to grow up, so that he can have a silver back like his father's and a big chest that he can thump! First, though Pongo has to learn how grown-up gorillas survive in the jungle.

FURTHER LITERATURE

The Bear Who Didn't Like Honey
Barbara Maitland

Nancy No Size **Mary Hoffman**

Why Is The Sky Blue? **Sally Grindley**

The Aardvark Who Wasn't Sure **Jill Tomlinson**

Lesson One
❖ *Once There Were Giants*

Setting the scene Show the picture on the cover and ask,
What do you see? Who do you think the giants might be?

This story is written as though it was told by the toddler on the cover of the book.

Focus *As you listen to the story, think of all the changes you notice as the toddler grows up. At the end of the story I want you to tell me how you think the toddler feels about being the youngest and the smallest.*

 Share the text and the pictures with the children without discussion.

Comprehension *How do you think she felt about being the youngest? How did she feel when she was being scolded, when she was on mum's knee, when her mum didn't come back for her for a long time, when she was fighting, when she was a bride, when she was a giant?*

Spot the differences between the first picture in the book and the last. [There is an extra person in the picture, hair is greyer, towelling nappy on first picture, disposable nappy on last picture, etc.]

Style and use of language

At which point in the story did you realise the toddler was a girl?
[You will probably get lots of different answers.]

What is special about the way this story is told?
[Occasional rhythm, eg *I wouldn't play games and I called people names and upset the water on Millie Magee. She's the one with the towel. The one being scolded is me.*]

Invite the children to join in and listen to the rhythm.

Link with personal/ sensitive issues

What clues were there in the words and pictures that told you the girl was changing and growing? Which picture in particular told you the biggest change?
[Size, shape, hair, etc.]

How did all the family feel at the end?

Individual, pair or group work

• Re-read the list of feeling words.

• Draw yourself when you were small. How did you feel then?

• Draw yourself now. How do you feel now?

• Around each picture, write any words you can to describe your feelings. At the bottom write how you have changed.

I used to feel ....

Now I feel ....

- Older children can draw their lifelines:
  Draw a line across your page. The beginning of the line is
  when you were born and the end of the line is the age you
  are now. At different points above the line write things that
  have happened to you and some of the experiences you have
  had especially things which made a change to your life.
  Below the line, write the feelings you had.

Reflection   Bring the class together to share some of the feelings. Help
them notice how they can have different or confused feelings
about one thing and that feelings change over time.

Write on the board some feelings about things from the past
compared to the feelings now.

Learning to relate

Re-read the story.

Lesson Two
❖❖ *Penguin's Progress*

Setting the scene   *This story is about Otto, a penguin chick. He has to learn all about being a penguin and how that is different from other creatures. He discovers his place in the world of penguins and learns how to grow up.*

We have taken extracts from the story, but the whole story could be usefully read with a class over a number of sessions.

Focus   *As I read the first part of the story, try to get to know Otto and what kind of a character he is.*

Read the first few pages of Chapter One, up to *'Anyway you're all right now you've got me'.*

Comprehension   Discuss with the children what they have learned about Otto.

Re-focus   *Otto goes on to learn all about being a penguin chick, how he gets fed by the females, the 'Aunties', who have been fishing, and how to huddle together with the other chicks to keep warm. I am going to read the next chapter. At the end I want you to tell me all the ways in which Otto shows he is growing up.*

Read Chapter Four to the children.

Comprehension   *What are the ways in which Otto showed that he was growing up?*

What makes Emperor penguins special?

What are the good things about being this way?

What are the not-so-good things?

**Style and use
of language**   *What do you think the author was trying to teach us about ourselves? Can you tell me examples of how he did this through the characters in the book?*

Can you think of other books about animals that help us to think about the way we live? [eg *Watership Down, The Three Little Pigs, The Aardvark Who Wasn't Sure.*]

**Link with
personal/
sensitive issues**   Talk with the children about the responsibilities that come as you grow and grow up. What responsibilities do we have at school? Responsibilities come with every part of growing up, eg caring for our teeth, caring for our bodies, being able to reach things and taking care.

**Individual, pair
or group work**   • Write a charter of Otto's responsibilities.

• As a group, decide and write a charter of 'our responsibilities'.

This can be extended to a whole class activity by drawing up a charter of 'Our Class Responsibilities' for display in the classroom.

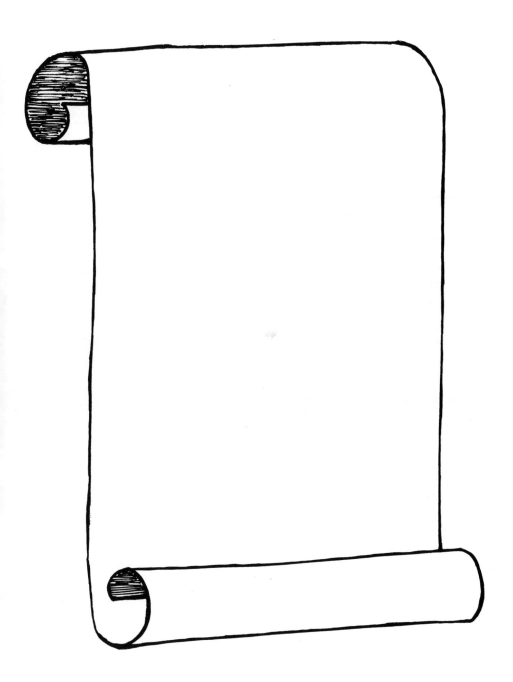

- Draw a set of stairs and write on each step the stages of Otto's growing up.

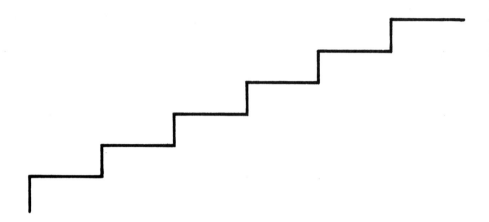

- Draw another set of stairs and write on each step the stages of you growing up.

Reflection   We all have responsibilities in the way we work together in this classroom.

Learning to relate

Re-read an extract the children would like to hear again and/or leave a copy of the book available for reading.

THEME THREE
FRIENDSHIPS AND RELATIONSHIPS

Learning to adjust

The skills of being together. What is a friend? What is a friendship? What is a family? Networks of relationships with old and young. Arrivals and departures.

SUGGESTED LITERATURE

Wilfrid Gordon McDonald Partridge
Mem Fox ❖

The relationships between young and old. Wilfrid Gordon McDonald Partridge is a small boy who has a big name - and that's why he likes Miss Nancy Delacourt Cooper, because she has a big name too. So when he finds Miss Nancy has lost her memory he determines to discover what a memory is so he can find it again for her.

This Is Our House
Michael Rosen ❖

George says the cardboard house is his and no-one else can play in it. But Lindy, Marly, Freddie, Charlene, Marlene, Luther, Sophie and Rasheda have other ideas! George learns a lesson about being left out and about including others.

Flour Babies
Anne Fine

When the annual school science fair comes round, Mr Cartright's class don't get to work on the Soap Factory, the Maggot Farm or the Exploding Custard Tins. To their intense disgust they get the Flour Babies - sweet little six-pound bags of flour that must be cared for at all times. Young Simon Martin, a committed hooligan, approaches the task with little enthusiasm. But as time passes, he grows fond of his flour baby and learns more than he ever could have imagined about the pressures and strains of relationships.

Little Beaver And The Echo
Amy MacDonald

Little Beaver lives all alone by the edge of the pond. He doesn't have any brothers. He doesn't have any sisters. Worst of all, he doesn't have any friends. One day, when he starts to cry, he hears someone else crying too, on the other side of his pond ... And so begins his touching quest for a friend.

The Suitcase Kid
Jacqueline Wilson

Ten-year-old Andy shares her experience of life after divorce in a realistic, but often very funny story. My family lived at Mulberry Cottage. Mum, Dad, me - and Radish, my Sylvanian rabbit. But now Mum lives with Bill the Baboon and his three kids. Dad lives with Carrie and her twins. And where do I live? I live out of a suitcase. One week with Mum's new family and one week with Dad's.

What Newt Could Do For Turtle
Jonathon London

Turtle is always helping Newt and saving him from danger. 'That's what friends are for', he says. But Newt feels embarrassed. If only there were something he could do to help Turtle.

FURTHER LITERATURE

Badger On The Barge **Janni Howker**
Something Else **Kathryn Cave**

Lesson One
❖ *Wilfrid Gordon McDonald Partridge*

Setting the scene *This story is about a small boy with a very long name whose house is next door to an old people's home. The boy knows all the people who live there.*

Focus *At the end of the story I want you to tell me what you know about the characters, the people in the book. And what do you know about the word 'memory'?*

 Read the text to the children without discussion.

Comprehension *What can you remember about the characters?*

What is memory? What's a memory? (Does everyone have the same answers to these questions?)

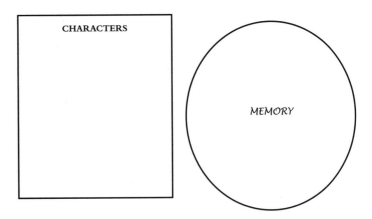

Why did Wilfrid Gordon particularly like Miss Nancy?

What did Wilfrid Gordon try to do? How did he do it?

What did Wilfrid Gordon think losing your memory was about?

How did Wilfrid Gordon and Miss Nancy feel at the end of the story?

Style and use of language

Look at the words used to describe the old people (eg Mrs Jordan who played the organ, Mr Tippet who was crazy about cricket). Did they help you remember them? How?

[Rhyme and each character was given something very individual.]

Did the words help you to have a picture in your head? How?

Link with personal/ sensitive issues

What was special about the friendship between Wilfrid Gordon and Miss Nancy?

What makes a special friend?

Wilfrid Gordon told Miss Nancy all his secrets. What do you think they might have been?

What secrets is it OK for us to keep and not keep?

This might also be an occasion to explain how Wilfrid Gordon's parents used the word 'lost' to mean forgetting some things from the past. Discuss other meanings of 'lost', eg objects can be lost, people can be lost when they go away or die.

Individual, pair or group work

- Write an advertisement for the 'Friend Wanted' column.

- Draw a basket. Inside it, write and/or draw any special memories you have. (Better still, take a real basket into class for children to put their memories in.)

- Choose one of the old people in the story and write about what you think they did, where they lived, etc, before they moved to the old people's home.

- Draw a special friend of yours. Write about what makes them special to you.

Reflection Bring the class together. We all have friends: some are old, some are young, some are special. It can hurt when we break friendships, but in this class we are all trying to be friendly with each other.

Learning to adjust

Re-read the story.

Lesson Two
❖ *This Is Our House*

**Setting
the scene** *This is a story about George who tells the other children that the cardboard house is his house and no one else can play in it.*

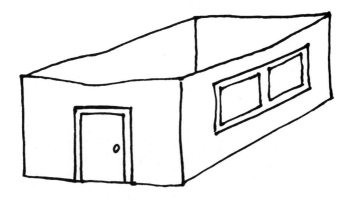

Focus *At the end of the story I want you to tell me all the different reasons you can remember that George gives for not letting anyone else play in the cardboard house.*

  Read the text to the children without discussion.

Comprehension *Let's go through all the reasons George gave for not letting anyone else play in the cardboard house.*

Why do you think he didn't want them to come in?

What were all the different things the other children tried so that they could get into the house?
[Straightforward request, pretending, using their imagination, and so on.]

What was the turning point in the story for George?

What did George do to try to get them to let him in?

Style and use of language

What did you notice about the pictures in the story?
[Particularly the colour and different layout of pages.]

Towards the end of the story, George was upset at being left out. What told you that things were going to change?

Link with personal/ sensitive issues

How do you think the children felt about being left out?

How did George feel when he was left out?

How do you feel when you are left out?

sad

angry

crying

Are there times when you have to share with other people when you don't want to? When? How does it feel? Does this help you to understand George's feelings?

Individual, pair or group work

- Re-read the vocabulary collected with the children.

- Take each of the words we have collected and write a sentence containing the word.

- Younger children may draw faces describing feeling words and add captions.

- Think of a time when you were left out or chose to be left out. Write five sentences to describe those times.

  I wanted to be on my own but ...

- Write down as many reasons as you can think of why people are sometimes left out of groups, eg they are smaller, don't wear the same clothes, etc.

- Give some reasons why people might want to play by themselves.

Reflection   Bring the class together. Being left out can be very hurtful. In this class we try to include everyone and take turns sharing with others.

Learning to adjust

 Re-read the story.

THEME FOUR
GRIEF, LOSS AND BEREAVEMENT

Learning that all feelings are OK

Losing things, finding things. Moving house, changing schools. Broken friendships. Family changes. Death.

SUGGESTED LITERATURE

Badger's Parting Gifts
Susan Varley ❖

When old Badger dies, his friends think they will be sad forever. But gradually they are able to remember Badger with joy and to treasure the gifts he left behind for every one of his friends. A sensitive book that can help children come to terms with the death of those they love.

The Bed And Breakfast Star
Jacqueline Wilson ❖❖

Elsa does her best to cheer her family up, but no-one seems to laugh any more - not since they lost their lovely house and had to move into a bed and breakfast hotel.

Badger On The Barge
Janni Howker

Miss Brady, who lives with a badger on her barge, draws her young friend, Helen, into a plot to defy the authorities. A story of the ways different encounters can change people's lives.

Grandma's Bill
Martin Waddell

With warmth and humour, Bill and Grandma look at photographs of the past and the present, and discover the reassuring sense of continuity and security they bring.

I'll Always Love You
Hans Wilhelm

The story of a boy and his best friend. All the family love Elfie, but the boy knows she's his dog. They do everything together. As the boy grows taller, Elfie gets rounder and slower, until one day she's not there any more. The young boy faces the loss of his companion, but remembers what he always told her: I'll always love you.

A New Home For Tiger
Joan Stimson

Moving home can be exciting. It can also be unsettling, especially when you're small. Moving means that everything is unfamiliar - Tiger doesn't like it. He takes himself back to his old home. Here, all alone, Tiger comes to understand that 'home' means many different things.

FURTHER LITERATURE

Emma's Lamb **Kim Lewis**

The Suitcase Kid **Jacqueline Wilson**

The Granny Project **Anne Fine**

First Snow **Kim Lewis**

Dear Daddy **Philippe Dupasquier**

Lesson One
❖ *Badger's Parting Gifts*

Setting the scene   *This is the story of Badger and his friends. Badger is growing very old.*

Focus   *At the end of the story I want you to tell me about all the gifts that Badger gave to the other animals in the story. Notice also how the other animals feel at the beginning of the story, in the middle and at the end.*

Read the text to the children without discussion.

Comprehension   *What were all the gifts Badger gave to the other animals?*

FROG
learning to skate

MRS RABBIT
making gingerbread rabbits

MOLE
cutting moles from paper

What was the 'very strange yet wonderful dream' Badger had?

What happened in the dream?

Which animal broke the news that Badger had died?

In the note Badger left, how did he describe dying?

What was Badger's only worry?

Re-read the page and collect words that describe the dream
and what was happening in the dream as badger went down
the long tunnel.

*Let's remember how the animals felt at three different times in the
story: at the beginning, in the middle and at the end.*

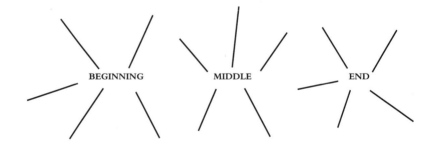

**Style and use
of language**

*How does the author use the seasons of the year to add to the
description of how the animals felt after Badger died?*

When do the animal's feelings start to change?

How do we know the animal's feelings are changing through the book?

**Link with
personal/
sensitive issues**

In which bit of the story did you feel saddest?

When did you begin to feel happier?

*What other feelings did you have as you listened to the story? Put
them under the four seasons of the year to help describe them.*

SUMMER	AUTUMN	WINTER	SPRING
----------	----------	----------	----------
----------	----------	----------	----------
----------	----------	----------	----------
----------	----------	----------	----------
----------	----------	----------	----------
----------	----------	----------	----------
----------	----------	----------	----------
----------	----------	----------	----------

Individual, pair or group work

· *The part of the story I will remember best is ... because ...*

· *The character I think felt the saddest was ... because ...*

· *If I moved away from this school, I would give these parting gifts to my friends ...*

Reflection Bring the class together. When we lose something, a pet, somebody, we often have a number of different feelings. They are all OK. It helps sometimes to have the memories or gifts that are left behind.

Learning that all feelings are OK

Re-read the story.

Lesson Two
❖❖ *The Bed And Breakfast Star*

Setting the scene   *I am going to read a short extract from 'The Bed And Breakfast Star' in which you will meet the chief character in the story, who is called Elsa. She is the one who tells the story.*

Focus   *As you listen to the first pages of the book, try to make pictures in your heads of Elsa, the person who tells the story, and her family. Also try to imagine each bed she has slept in and how she must have felt.*

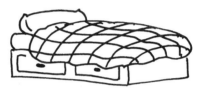

   Read the first few pages of the book up to '*Because he's thick. Thick, thick, thick as a brick*'.

Comprehension   *List all the members of Elsa's family.*

How do you think each looked and behaved?

How did Elsa feel about each of them?

Invite the children to imagine how Elsa turned her cot into a play house, a car and a castle.

Did Elsa think her mother's joke about leaving her behind in hospital was funny? Why / Why not?

Why did people say Elsa was 'a bed and breakfast star'? How did she feel about that?

The rest of the book tells the story of how Elsa and her family came to live in a bed and breakfast hotel. From what you know of Elsa already, how do you think this story is going to develop and end? Is there anything that makes you think it could have a happy ending?

Style and Use of Language

*This story is told by Elsa, in what we call the **first person**. She seems to be talking straight to you, the reader. Do you enjoy this kind of writing? What other ways of writing are there? Are there advantages in each way?*

How did the author tell you that Elsa had a sense of humour?

SENSE OF HUMOUR

- *her duvet dress*
- *cornflake curls*
- *two fried eggs for eyes*
- *streaky bacon smile*
- *her description of Hank*

There are some things Elsa can joke about using a lot of words. What?
[her name, for example]

There are some things she doesn't joke about and explain. What?
[for example, her feelings about her Dad]

The author uses word pictures to describe what people are like. Can you find a word picture so good that you could do a drawing from it?
You might like to introduce the idea of a **character study**.

Does the author make you want to read on and find out what happened to them all? How does she do this?

Link with personal/ sensitive issues

Talk with the children about how it feels when someone you care about moves away. Collect some of their vocabulary of loss. Ask the children to think of how it feels when you know that person won't come back. Talk about how important it is to share your feelings with someone. Ask them to think how they could help themselves or someone else who is feeling this way.

Think about Elsa and her family, who have lost their home. What does Elsa do to help herself and help the others?

Do you ever joke about something you feel that isn't really funny? Why do people do this?
[Because they're embarrassed, they don't want to cry in front of other people, etc.]

Individual, pair or group work

- Draw two windows – one open and one closed. Around or in the open window, write words describing Elsa's outwards feelings and around or in the closed window, words describing her inner feelings.

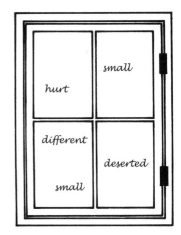

- Working in pairs or small groups, draw an outline to represent Elsa.

  What do you know or imagine about Elsa? Write these on or around your outline, eg physical appearance, personality, likes, dislikes, hopes, dreams, fears, people around her.

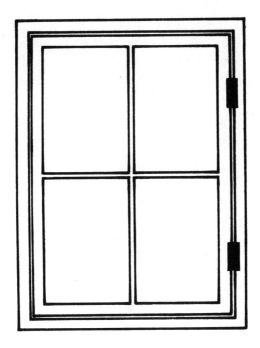

Reflection Bring the drawings together to share and discuss.

Remind the class that all feelings are OK and that people are helped by sharing their feelings. How can we, as a class, recognise our own and other people's feelings and treat them with respect? Can we decide how we show our feelings?

Learning that all feelings are OK

You may wish to read further extracts from the book or make it available for children to read for themselves.

THEME FIVE
FEARS

Learning to strive and overcome

Spoken and unspoken. Fantasy and reality. Hopes and dreams.

SUGGESTED LITERATURE

Not Now, Bernard
David McKee   ❖

Bernard can't find a way to make his parents stop and listen to what he is saying: there is a monster in his garden.

Don't Forget To Write
Martina Selway   ❖ ❖

This is a variation of an old and loved theme. A little girl is sent to stay on a farm and protests strongly. She is told to brush her hair, wash, clean her teeth and mostly 'don't forget to write'. Her letters form the text of the book. At first she is homesick but gradually this changes, until finally she is reluctant to go home.

Can't You Sleep, Little Bear?
Martin Waddell

Little Bear is frightened of the dark so that when it comes to bedtime he can't get to sleep - not even with the biggest lantern of them all at his bedside. Fortunately Big Bear finds a most ingenious way to reassure him.

You're Safe Now, Waterdog
Richard Edwards

This is the story of a favourite toy, who is loved, forgotten about, and then loved all over again when he is rescued by a little girl called Hattie.

Goodnight Mister Tom
Michelle Magorian

Willie Beech is a sad, deprived child evacuated to an alien country community during the second World War. He slowly learns to cope with the changes and conflicting emotions in his life, including the death of his best friend whose cheerful personality has been a key element in Willie's development.

The Owl Who Was Afraid Of The Dark
Jill Tomlinson

Plop is exactly the same as every baby barn owl that has ever been - except for one thing. Plop is afraid of the dark. His parents keep telling him that dark is best, but it's no use. Plop just wants to be a day bird. Finally, his mother pushes him out of the nest to ask other people what they think of the dark and Plop is amazed by their replies.

FURTHER LITERATURE

The Bear Who Didn't Like Honey
Barbara Maitland

We're Going On A Bear Hunt Michael Rosen

Lollopy Joyce Dunbar

The Whale's Song Dyan Sheldon

Lesson One
❖ *Not Now, Bernard*

Setting
the scene
This story is about Bernard, a little boy who wants to tell his Mum and Dad that there's a monster in the garden.

Focus
At the end of the story we'll talk about the things that both the monster and Bernard did and said to his Mum and Dad to try to make them listen.

Read the text to the children without discussion.

Comprehension
Did Bernard's parents listen to him? Did they listen to the monster? How do you know?

What did Bernard say and do to try to get Mum and Dad to turn around and listen?

What did the monster say and do?

> **MONSTER**
>
> - roared
> - bit
> - ate Bernard's dinner

Style and use
of language
What do Bernard's parents keep saying? How many different ways can you say it?

Invite the class to try out the different ways with you.

How does the author show in his pictures what people were thinking?

From the illustrations how do you think the monster feels?

angry   surprised   bemused   curious   defeated

**Link with
personal/
sensitive issues**

How do we get someone to listen?
How do I get you to listen?
How do you get me to listen to you?

*We don't want our classroom to be a 'Not Now, Bernard' classroom.
Can we have a key word or question which we could use when we
wanted to tell each other something and we think the other person isn't
listening?*

You could invite the children to think of ideas for this during
their individual, pair or group work, eg 'Can I have a Bernard
minute?'

**Individual, pair
or group work**

- *I think Bernard's fears and worries were about ...
      and if his Mum and Dad had listened to him ...*

- *When I was younger I sometimes worried about ...*

- Can you think of a class motto which will help us listen to
  each other? Draw this on a shield.

Reflection

Bring the class together. Review class work.

Sometimes our fears and worries can feel like monsters. It can
help sometimes to share these worries. In this class we want to
try and listen to each other and help each other to overcome
any worries and fears we might have.

Learning to strive and overcome

Re-read the story.

Lesson Two
❖❖ *Don't Forget To Write*

Setting the scene   *This story is about a little girl who is sent to stay on a farm and is told 'Don't forget to write'. At first she is homesick, but gradually her feelings change. Each page is a letter she writes home.*

This is an opportunity to introduce the way in which writers sometimes use letters as a means of writing a book.

Focus   *At the end, I want you to tell me the clues you were given that Rosie was changing her mind about wanting to go home.*

   Read the text to the children.

Comprehension   *What were the clues you picked up about Rosie changing her mind?*

Grandpa sounds as though he teases. Can you tell me an example? [When he says that the tooth fairies hadn't been to their house for so long they might have forgotten the way, etc.]

What did Grandpa mean when he said, about the tooth fairy money, 'It'll have to burn a hole in your pocket?'

What did it mean when 'the auctioneer spoke so fast it sounded like gobbledegook?'

Aunt Mabel sounded a bit cross at first. When did she begin to change?

Style and use of language   *Do you feel we got to know Rosie through her letters? How?*

What do you like about this style of writing through letters? What do you not like?

Link with personal/ sensitive issues Talk about Rosie's pet name.

Did she like being called 'Ginger Nut'? Why not? Are some nicknames cruel and some loving? Should we use people's nicknames without their permission? Is it OK to shorten names or change them?

Rosie didn't tell Grandpa she didn't like the name, she wrote it to him. How could she have told him? How can you tell someone that you don't like the name they are calling you?

Sometimes it is difficult to tell people things we don't like or to share our fears and worries with them. What can help?

Individual, pair or group work
- Write a letter to someone who doesn't know you. Write about yourself to help your new pen friend get to know you.

  Any theme can be used for the letter. With younger children the teacher can act as a scribe and the children can write a letter about the class as a whole.

- Think about the fear and worries someone a little younger than you might have. Make a list. Choose one (or more) items from your list and write down what you think may help them overcome their fear or worry. Who might be able to help them?

Reflection Bring the class together to share some of their work.

Learning to strive and overcome

 Re-read a letter from the book that the children would like to hear again.

THEME SIX
BEING SAFE, STAYING SAFE

Learning to be aware

Safe bodies. Safe feelings. Safe places. Safe people.

SUGGESTED LITERATURE

Stranger Danger
Anne Fine   ❖

Joe is confused. Never take sweets from a stranger and Never go with a stranger are the two safety rules the nice policeman gave them. But it's not that easy! In the concert hall, Joe finds he can't stop coughing. Should he take a peppermint from the kind looking gentleman behind him? Joe soon discovers that a little common sense comes in handy.

The Egg Man
from *Badger On The Barge*
Janni Howker   ❖❖

Two characters double dare each other to visit the old man in his house, stopping with will you tell your Mum and Dad? This story raises issues around personal safety and dangers. However, the issues mostly raised are around the importance of telling: Where are you going? Who with? What happened?

The Huge Bag Of Worries
Virginia Ironside

Wherever Jenny goes, her worries follow her - in a big blue bag! They are there when she goes swimming, when she is watching TV, even when she is in the lavatory. Jenny decides they will have to go. But who can she get to help her?

I'll Take You To Mrs Cole
Nigel Gray

The story of two families, two homes and a young boy's changing perceptions of family life. He visits the other family. How did he know it was safe? Why did he venture in?

Two Monsters
David McKee

Reconciling differences. Two monsters, who both think they are absolutely 'right' come to understand that they can both be right, but they destroy the mountain in the process.

The Year Of The Worm
Ann Pilling

Peter Wrigley hasn't got an awful lot going for him. Timid, puny and unpopular, he's the perfect butt for school bullies and certainly seems to earn the nickname 'worm'. He never feels really safe.

FURTHER LITERATURE

The Very Hungry Caterpillar **Eric Carle**

Six Dinner Sid **Inga Moore**

Lesson One
❖ *Stranger Danger*

Setting the scene   *This is a story about Joe who listens to a talk by a police officer on safety rules. Joe is left with some confusions and faces a series of dilemmas.*

Focus   *I am going to read you the first part of the story where Joe listens to the talk on safety rules. At the end I want you to tell me what the safety rules were.*

 Read Chapter One to the children without discussion.

Comprehension   Collect the safety rules.

> **SAFETY RULES**

Style and use of language   *Was there anything you found amusing or funny in the story?*

In Chapter One, why do you think the author used the piece about the daddy-long-legs?

Re-focus   *As I read the next chapter try to think about what Joe is feeling and thinking. At the end I will ask you to tell me what you think his thoughts and feelings are.*

Read Chapter Two to the children without discussion.

Comprehension   *What was Joe thinking and feeling?*

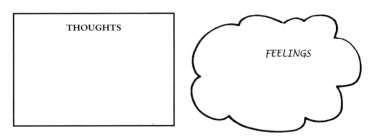

When the lady came into the classroom to get Joe, why did Joe think she was beginning to get impatient with him?

Why was Joe first on her list?

Was Joe pleased or reluctant to go with the lady? How do you know?

Did he say 'Stranger Danger'? Why not?

Style and use of language   *At what point did you begin to think Joe would go with the lady? Why was that?*

Was there anything you found funny or amusing in this chapter?

Collect ideas and add them to the list from Chapter One.

Link with personal/ sensitive issues   *Can you think of any situations where you have had similar thoughts and feelings to Joe? What was the situation? How did you feel?*

Individual, pair or group work
- Think about what you know or imagine you know about Joe so far. In your group, draw an outline to represent Joe and write and draw on anything you know or imagine. We are going to build up our pictures of Joe as we read through the book.

  Bring the class together to share pictures.

Refocus   *At the end of the next chapter I want you to tell me what you know or imagine about Joe's family. In this chapter Joe has to make a difficult decision – try to think about how he was feeling and how he made his final decision.*

Read Chapter Three to the children without discussion.

Comprehension   *Who do you now know was in Joe's family?*

What do you know about them?

What was the decision Joe had to make?

How did he make his final decision?

How was he feeling?

FEELINGS

Style and use of language

What sort of word picture did the author give you of the theatre?

Why do you think he chose these words?

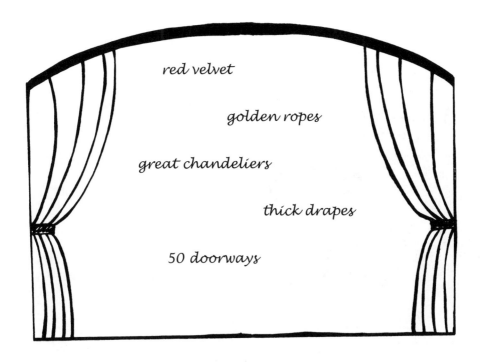

red velvet

golden ropes

great chandeliers

thick drapes

50 doorways

How did the author use humour in this chapter?
Add to the list.

Link with personal/ sensitive issues

Can you think of times when you have had similar feelings to Joe?

Do colours remind you of feelings? Which colour? What feeling?

COLOURS	FEELINGS
Red	
Blue	
Yellow	

What can help us manage our feelings?

Individual, pair or group work

- Add to your outline of Joe anything else you know about him and his family from Chapter Three.

- Draw yourself and write the names of the people in your family around you.

- Draw yourself and write and draw the important things about being you.

Re-focus

In this final chapter, Joe faces another difficult decision. At the end I want you to tell me about the situation, what decision he made and what Nana and Grandpa said about his decision.

 Read Chapter Four to the children without discussion.

Comprehension

Review the focus questions.

Style and use of language

Are there any more bits you thought were amusing or funny to add to our list?

How does the author reinforce messages about safety rules in this chapter?

How do you feel at the end of the book? Do you think this is what the author intended?

Link with personal/ sensitive issues

We all face difficult situations and decisions at different times in our lives. In Chapter Four we were told that the good thing about safety rules is they remind us to stop and think and use our common sense. It's a bit like traffic lights.

Draw traffic lights on the board.

STOP

THINK

DECIDE

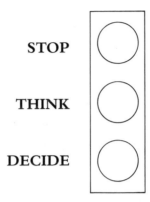

Can you give me an example of a difficult situation someone your age might be faced with?
Write the situation against red light.

What would that person's choices be when the light was on amber?
Write the choices alongside the amber light.

What do you think the best decision would be from those choices? Why?
Write the decision against the green light.

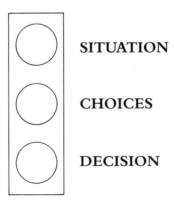

SITUATION

CHOICES

DECISION

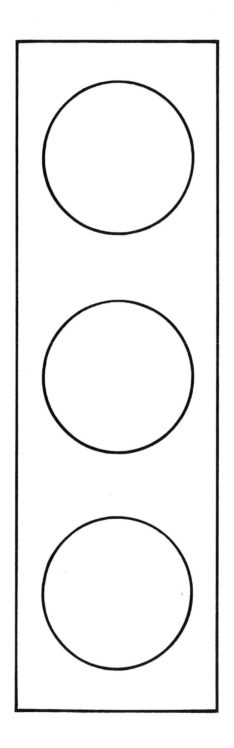

Individual, pair or group work

- Think of a situation someone younger than you might be faced with. Draw a set of traffic lights.

  Write the situation alongside the red light, the choices alongside the amber light, and alongside the green light write what the best choice would be and why.

  Now do the same for someone your own age using a different situation.

  Now do the same for someone a little bit older than you.

- Is there anything else you would like to add to your picture of Joe? This is your last chance.

Reflection

Bring the class together to share some of the traffic light situations.

Display the final outlines of Joe and let everyone look at them all. Discuss any similarities and differences.

Review the author's use of humour through the book. Is this a good way of helping people to take notice of safety messages?

We need to be responsible for keeping ourselves safe. We are learning to be aware of difficult situations and decisions.

Learning to be aware

Re-read a chapter of the story and/or make a copy of the book available for individual reading.

Lesson Two

❖❖ *The Egg Man* from *Badger On The Barge*

Setting the scene
This is the story of two girls, Bridget and Jane, who dare, double dare and double double dare each other to visit Mr Black, the old Egg Man, in his cottage at the edge of the village. There has always been a rumour that Mr Black murdered his wife, Nell, a long time ago. Bridget and Jane have already been to his cottage when he was out and had a look round inside. They were almost caught there by him when he came back in his van. This time, however, they plan to meet him, pretending they have come to buy some eggs.

Focus
While listening to this extract, decide which of the two girls was the more sensible and aware of the risks they were taking. Which one was more sensitive to Mr Black's feelings and tried to understand him?

Read the text to the children without discussion.
Take the extract from about half way through Chapter Three from '*They went up by the side of the house, openly, in view ...*' to just into Chapter Four, '*Will you tell your Mum and Dad ...*'.

Comprehension
Collect answers to the focus question. Encourage the children to recall both the situation and the words used.

BRIDGET	JANE
Sensible	Sensitive
'Let's go.'	Found excuses for
'No thanks. We	him.
can't stay for tea.'	Shook hands.
Walked away.	'He's just old. He
Shouted to Jane.	thought I was
	Nellen ...'
	Went with him.
	She was sad for him.
	She knew he wouldn't
	harm her.

Collect words and phrases for a word picture of Mr Black.

Which words best describe his appearance? Which words would best help an artist draw him?

Which words would help you to play his part if you were an actor taking part in a TV performance?

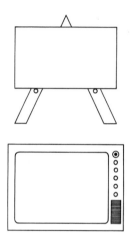

MR BLACK

scratched and broken spectacles
white stubble
flakey skin
wrinkled cheeks
tatty jacket
clumsy
gentle
whispery laugh
hands light yet sharp as pencils
ugly, bewildered old face

Style and use of language *How did the author build up the silence? What things is silence compared to?*

Which words helped us share what was happening to Jane?

SILENCE	WHAT WAS HAPPENING TO JANE
like a grey cloud wrapping them back	like shaking the cold claw of a dead sparrow
like dust settling	the egg man had pinned her ... to the ribbon
like autumn leaves	

Remind children what a **simile** is and why it is used. Ask the children to listen for examples of similes in the re-reading at the end of the lesson.

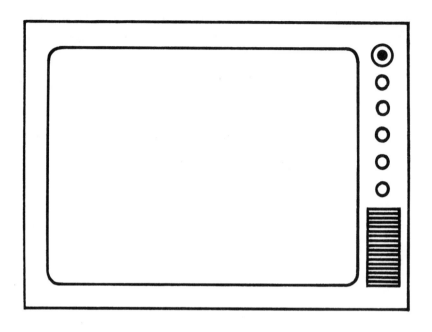

Link with personal/ sensitive issues

Which were the moments in the story where the two girls could have made a different decision? How would these different decisions have changed the way the story went?

Ask the class to think about Bridget's approach, of seeing a possible danger and walking away. Compare that to Jane's concern for not hurting the old man's feelings. Encourage the children to put themselves into a middle ground. Could Bridget have been more caring about the Egg Man's feelings? Could Jane have been more aware of the possible dangers? How would this have changed the way they behaved?

Return to the last line in the extract where Bridget says, *'Will you tell your Mum and Dad?'* Ask the children to decide whether they would tell their parents and how Jane might tackle telling *her* parents. What would she say?

Individual, pair or group work

• Work individually and draw Jane. Draw a speech bubble and write in it what you think Jane would say to make her Mum or Dad stop and listen to her.

• Compare and share ideas. Can the children agree on one form of words?

Reflection Remind the class that being aware of their own and other people's feelings is part of being safe, as is being aware of dangerous situations.

Learning to be aware

Re-read the extract, listening for and enjoying the word pictures.

Make the book available for those children who want to know how Jane told her parents.

TALKING ABOUT FEELINGS

Learning to communicate

Naming feelings, sharing feelings, managing feelings. Understanding other people's feelings. Different people feeling different things.

SUGGESTED LITERATURE

The True Story Of The Three Little Pigs
Jon Scieszka ❖

You may think you know the story of the 3 little pigs and the big bad wolf – but are you sure you know the real story? This is the story as told by A. Wolf who tell his tale and his feelings.

Red Sky In The Morning
Elizabeth Laird ❖ ❖

Anna is a young teenager whose parents are having a baby quite late in their lives. Anna is looking forward to the baby coming and she thinks it will give her a chance to show all the family how grown up she is. Ben is born with hydrocephalus and Anna finds herself full of love for him and teaches him things a step at a time. She wants her school friends and strangers to know that her brother is beautiful, funny and clever in his own special way, but finds this is very difficult.

John Brown, Rose & The Midnight Cat
Jenny Wagner

Rose lived with her dog, John Brown. We are all right, John Brown, said Rose. Just the two of us, you and me. But she reckoned without the mysterious midnight cat, and it was John Brown who realised that things were going to change.

The Whale's Song
Dyan Sheldon

A story of imagination and longing as a young girl's dreams come true.

Poems About Feelings
Selected by A Earl & D Sensier

From bad mood days to saying sorry, staying up late and first day at school nerves, this selection of poems about feelings draws on verse from all over the world.

When Grandma Came
Jill Paton Walsh

When Grandma visits Madeleine she tells of her travels to exotic lands and of the wonders she has seen. But there is nothing in all creation quite like Madeleine herself.

FURTHER LITERATURE

Wilfrid Gordon McDonald Partridge **Mem Fox**

Grandma's Bill **Martin Waddell**

Flour Babies **Anne Fine**

Lesson One
❖ *The True Story Of The Three Little Pigs*

Setting the scene

Do you remember the story of 'The Three Little Pigs'? Tell me what you remember about it.

Give a recap of the story if necessary.

This is a story called 'The True Story Of The Three Little Pigs', and it is told by a wolf.

Focus

At the end of the story, I want you to tell me what you know or imagine about the wolf and his feelings.

 Read the text to the children.

Comprehension

Invite the children to share what they know or imagine about the wolf and build up a picture of what he is like.

You might like to remind them here of the concept of a **character study**.

His name ...
He eats ...
His family ...
His health ...
His feelings ...

Style and use of language

In what ways does the author use humour in the story?

Did you enjoy the way the story was written?

Do you know why?

Do you know what it is called when a story is written in this way?

What nationality would you guess the author is? Why?

It could be useful to discuss styles in relation to nationalities and accents and dialects.

The other characters in this book were the three little pigs. What does the wolf think about each one? What does he tell us about each one?

Link with personal/ sensitive issues

Why did the wolf think he might have got his reputation as being a 'Big, Bad Wolf'.
[Because of what he eats.]

What does he eat?

What kinds of things do people get a 'bad' reputation for? What kinds of things do people get a 'good' reputation for?

This story had two sides to it, the wolf's side and the three little pigs' side. When something happens or when people get a reputation for something they have done, are there always two sides to a story?

Do you always feel able to give your side of a story? What helps you? What stops you?

Individual, pair or group work

- Imagine you are someone who bullies other people. Write a paragraph (or more) written by A. Bully, giving your side of the story and your feelings.

- Make a list of reasons 'for' and 'against' believing the wolf.

FOR	AGAINST
....	....
....	....
....	....
....	....
....	....

- If you had to choose, whose story would you believe – the wolf's or the pigs'? Why?

- One person in the group speaks on behalf of the wolf and one person speaks on behalf of the pigs. Take it in turns to try and convince the rest of the group that your side of the story is the right one.

  Two or more children in turn can speak for each side. The group decides who they believe and why.

  Review as a whole class.

- Whole class activity. Divide the class in half. One half debates on behalf of the wolf telling the true story and the other half on behalf of the pigs. Control the debate by giving the class the rule that only the person holding the talking object, eg a pen, can speak - move the debate along by ensuring that the pen is passed between the two sides. At the end, vote on which story is the most believable.

WOLF   **PIGS**

Reflection Everyone has feelings, even if sometimes people don't show them. In this class we will try to consider people's feelings and listen to their point of view. We will try not to blame other people for things that happen, but help each other instead.

Learning to communicate

 Re-read the story.

Lesson Two

❖❖ *Red Sky In The Morning*

Setting the scene   *This is a story about Anna, a young teenager, whose parents are having a baby quite late in their lives. Anna is looking forward to the baby coming. She thinks it will give her a chance to show all the family how grown up she is.*

Ben is born with hydrocephalus and Anna finds herself full of love for him. She teaches him things one step at a time. She wants her school friends and strangers to know that her brother is beautiful, funny and clever in his own special way, but finds this is very difficult.

I am going to read a short extract from the story.

Focus   *I want you to tell me, at the end of the reading, how Anna felt about her brother, and what made her angry. Who is the one person she trusts? Why?*

 Read the extract to the children starting about halfway through Chapter Three at '*I used to feel like a gladiator*', and finishing about four pages into Chapter Four at '*People seemed to like me more, not less*'.

Comprehension   Collect the children's answers to the focus questions.

ANNA'S FEELINGS ABOUT BEN	ANNA WAS ANGRY BECAUSE ...	ANNA TRUSTED MRS CHAPMAN BECAUSE ...

What was Anna ashamed of?

What was the best bit of advice that Mrs Chapman gave to Anna, do you think?

Ask the children how they think the story will develop. Collect their ideas for later discussion.

Style and use of language
Think about Anna when her friends were all listening to Miranda describing Ben. What were Miranda's words?

How would you have felt if you had been one of the group listening?

How would you have felt if Ben had been your brother?

Do you think Anna did the right thing?

How did the author describe the children as they listened to Miranda? Recall some of the language used:

agog with curiosity
not a drop of the milk of human kindness
riveting attention   *How can attention be like a rivet?*

There were two or three phrases to describe Anna's feelings, those which made her act so angrily. Recall them or re-read the paragraph

something clicked   *What clicked?*
a magnificent anger   *Can anger be magnificent?*
an iron calm   *Can calm be iron?*

Look at the way the author builds up the anger. Did you guess that Anna would end up in tears? What clues did you have?

Look at other examples of metaphorical language and how they add to the tension. Explore the idea and other examples of **metaphor.**

each piece of chocolate an olive branch
a great burden rolled off my shoulders

Link with personal/ sensitive issues

Use the extract when Anna was listening to Miranda describing Ben to consider the central sensitive issue of disability or, as Anna viewed it, Ben's special abilities.

Explore the tension between Anna wanting her friends to understand Ben's disabilities and not wanting her friends to label her because of him.

Talk about how the strangers reacted to Ben. Ask the children to suggest more understanding ways of behaving.

Individual, pair or group work

• What 'labels' do people give to other people? Write down as many as you can think of.
[eg stupid, swot, fatty, four-eyes.]
Why do you think people label other people?

• Write down as many emotions or 'feeling' words' as you can think of. Choose five of the words and write a sentence describing a time when you felt that feeling.

I felt sad when ...

I felt really happy when ...

• Build a 'feeling wall' in the classroom. Write each feeling word on a piece of sideways A4 paper. Each piece of paper becomes a brick in the wall and children can refer to the wall to find words to describe how they feel about an event, activity, etc. More words can be added over the term.

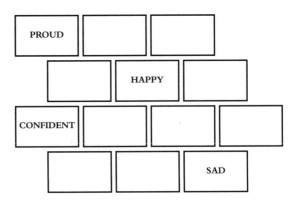

Reflection Bring the class together and reflect on the impact of strong feelings on our behaviour and how anger, fear, and relief make us do things we might not normally do. We do not always have a choice about how we feel, but we do have a choice about our actions and behaviour as a result of our feelings. We are responsible for our own behaviour.

Reflect too on how much Anna's friends learned from her that day and how much she learned from Ben's love of life, even though that life was so short.

Learning to communicate

You may wish to read further extracts, particularly those which deal with Ben's death and Anna's grief and loss.

Chapter 10, tells the story of how Ben gets a bad attack of flu and dies.

Chapter 11 deals with Anna's first experience of a funeral.

On the final page she remembers Ben with love.

RECOMMENDED LITERATURE

THEME	TITLE	AUTHOR(S)	PUBLISHER	DATE	ISBN
4	*A New Home For Tiger*	Joan Stimson	Scholastic Children's Books	1996	0-590-54194-3
1	*A Piece of Cake*	Jill Murphy	Walker Books Ltd	1994	0-7445-3735-5
1	*Amazing Grace*	Mary Hoffman	Frances Lincoln Ltd	1991	0-7112-0699-6
3/4	*Badger On The Barge*	Janni Howker	Heinemann Educational	1987	0-435-12313-0
4★	*Badger's Parting Gifts*	Susan Varley	Picture Lions	1992	0-00-664317-5
1	*Bill's New Frock*	Anne Fine	Mammoth Books	1990	0-7497-0305-9
5	*Can't You Sleep, Little Bear?*	Martin Waddell	Walker Books Ltd	1990	0-7445-1316-2
1★	*Comfort Herself*	Geraldine Kaye	Scholastic Children's Books	1984	0-590-19074-1
1	*Coming Into My Tropical Garden* (Poetry)	Grace Nicols	Black	1988	0-7136-2989-4
4	*Dear Daddy*	Philippe Dupasquier	Penguin Books Ltd	1986	0-14-050540-7
5★	*Don't Forget To Write*	Martina Selway	Random House	1991	0-09-920681-1
2/4	*Emma's Lamb*	Kim Lewis	Walker Books Ltd	1992	0-7445-2031-2
4	*First Snow*	Kim Lewis	Walker Books	1993	0-7445-4325-8
1	*Five Minutes' Peace*	Jill Murphy	Walker Books Ltd	1989	0-7445-1363-4
3/7	*Flour Babies*	Anne Fine	Penguin Books Ltd	1994	0-14-036147-2
5	*Goodnight Mister Tom*	Michelle Magorian	Penguin Books Ltd	1981	0-14-037233-4
4/7	*Grandma's Bill*	Martin Waddell	McDonanld Young Books	1997	0-7500-0307-3
2	*Growing Pains*	Jenny Stow	Frances Lincoln Ltd	1995	0-7112-0955-3
4	*I'll Always Love You*	Hans Wilhelm	Hodder Children's Books	1985	0-340-40153-2
6	*I'll Take You To Mrs Cole*	Nigel Gray	Andersen Press Ltd	1987	0-86264-105-5
7	*John Brown, Rose & The Midnight Cat*	Jenny Wagner	Penguin Books Ltd	1979	0-14-050306-4
3	*Little Beaver And The Echo*	Amy MacDonald	Walker Books Ltd	1990	0-7445-0443-0
5	*Lollopy*	Joyce Dunbar	Picture Lions	1993	0-00664-187-3
2	*Nancy No Size*	Mary Hoffman	Mammoth Books	1990	0-7497-0090-4
2	*Nearly But Not Quite*	Paul Rogers	Bodley Head Children's Books	1997	0-370-32423-4
5★	*Not Now, Bernard*	David McKee	Random House	1990	0-09-924050-5
1	*Nothing*	Mick Inkpen	Hodder Children's Books	1995	0-340-62650-0
2★	*Once There Were Giants*	Martin Waddell	Walker Books Ltd	1989	0-7445-1791-5
2★	*Penguin's Progress*	Jill Tomlinson	Mammoth Books	1990	0-7497-0867-0
7	*Poems About Feelings*	Selected by A Earl & D Sensier	Wayland	1994	0-7502-0972-0
7★	*Red Sky In The Morning*	Elizabeth Laird	Macmillan Children's Books	1997	0-434-94718-8
1★/6	*Six Dinner Sid*	Inga Moore	McDonald Young Books	1996	0-7500-0304-9
1/3	*Something Else*	Kathryn Cave	Penguin Books Ltd	1994	0-670-84892-1

RECOMMENDED LITERATURE

THEME	TITLE	AUTHOR(S)	PUBLISHER	DATE	ISBN
6★	Stranger Danger	Anne Fine	Penguin Books Ltd	1991	0-14-034302-4
2	The Aardvark Who Wasn't Sure	Jill Tomlinson	Mammoth	1991	0-7497-0863-8
2/5	The Bear Who Didn't Like Honey	Barbara Maitland	All Books For Children	1996	1-85406-236-0
4★	The Bed And Breakfast Star	Jacqueline Wilson	Transworld Publishers Ltd	1995	0-440-86324-4
6★	The Egg Man from Badger On The Barge	Janni Howker	Heinemann Educational	1987	0-435-12313-0
2	The Gorilla Who Wanted To Grow Up	Jill Tomlinson	Mammoth Books	1991	0-7497-0865-4
4	The Granny Project	Anne Fine	Mammoth Books	1990	0-7497-0186-2
6	The Huge Bag Of Worries	Virginia Ironside	McDonald Young Books	1996	0-7500-2124-1
5	The Owl Who Was Afraid Of The Dark	Jill Tomlinson	Mammoth Books	1992	0-7497-0795-x
3/4	The Suitcase Kid	Jacqueline Wilson	Transworld Publishers	1993	0-440-86311-2
7★	The True Story Of The Three Little Pigs	Jon Scieszka	Penguin Books Ltd	1991	0-14-054056-3
p9	The Velveteen Rabbit	Margery Williams	Heinemann Educational	1991	0-434-97265-7
6	The Very Hungry Caterpillar	Eric Carle	Penguin Books Ltd	1974	0-14-050087-1
5/7	The Whale's Song	Dyan Sheldon	Random House	1993	0-09-973760-4
6	The Year Of The Worm	Ann Pilling	Penguin Books Ltd	1985	0-14-031821-6
3★	This Is Our House	Michael Rosen	Walker Books Ltd	1996	0-7445-3750-9
6	Two Monsters	David McKee	Random House	1991	0-09-945530-7
5	We're Going On A Bear Hunt	Michael Rosen	Walker Books Ltd	1989	0-7445-2323-0
3	What Newt Could Do For Turtle	Jonathon London	Walker Books Ltd	1996	0-7445-3271-x
1/7	When Grandma Came	Jill Paton Walsh	Penguin Books Ltd	1993	0-14-054327-9
2	Why Is The Sky Blue?	Sally Grindley	Andersen Press Ltd	1996	0-86264-691-x
3★/7	Wilfrid Gordon McDonald Partridge	Mem Fox	Penguin Books Ltd	1987	0-14-050586-5
5	You're Safe Now, Waterdog	Richard Edwards	Orion Children's Books	1996	1-85881-279-8

THEMES

1 Being me, being you • **2 Growing and growing up** • **3 Friendships and relationships**
4 Grief, loss and bereavement • **5 Fears** • **6 Being safe, staying safe** • **7 Talking about feelings**

3★ = Lesson plan • **3** = Synopsis • 3 = Further recommended literature